VOLLEYBALL

WRITTEN BY CHRISTIE COSTANZO

ROURKE CORPORATION, INC.
VERO BEACH, FLORIDA 32964

PRO-AM SPORTS

The Rourke Corporation, Inc.
P.O. Box 3328, Vero Beach, FL 32964

Costanzo, Christie.
  Volleyball/by Christie Costanzo.
     p. cm.—(Pro-am sports)
  Includes bibliographical references (p.);
  ISBN 0-86593-344-8
  1. Volleyball–Juvenile literature. I. Title. II. Series.
  GV1015.3C67 1993
  796.325–dc20   93-27153
                                        CIP
                                        AC

Cover photograph: *Volleyball Monthly*
Interior Photographs:
Allsport USA 4; 22 (Richard Martin/Agence Vandystat);
34, 35 (Tony Duffy); 42 (Mike Powell)
Christie Costanzo 8, 12, 15, 24, 31, 39, 40
Pepperdine University 37
Sideout Sport 28
United States Volleyball Association 10, 13, 17, 38
Volleyball Monthly 6, 9, 18, 20, 25, 32

Series Editor: Gregory Lee
Book design and production:
      The Creative Spark, San Clemente, CA

Printed in the USA

VOLLEYBALL

A versatile game that can be played with two, four, or six players, volleyball has become a highly competitive sport.

CONTENTS

HOT TIP:
To learn how to dig a low ball, turn to page 6.

Volleyball is one of the fastest, most exciting team sports that appeals to men and women, young and old alike.

This is Volleyball

CHAPTER ONE

It could be the final point in a five-game match against two rival volleyball teams. The match score is tied at two games apiece. The winner of this game wins it all. It's game point and the referee signals the server by blowing the whistle.

The six players on the opposite court lean slightly forward on the balls of their feet in anticipation of the serve. The server lightly tosses the ball into the air, then leaps up and smashes it across to the other side of the court.

A back-row player makes a perfect pass up to the setter who, with arms stretched overhead, lightly sets the ball to the waiting hitter. The hitter takes two steps and then leaps into the air, pounding the ball down on the other side of the court.

The ball makes it past the block at the net and looks as if it will hit the ground until a small quick player in the back makes a body-sacrificing dive. With arms extended out as far as they will go, the player just manages to dig the ball up to the net, saving the play. The crowd screams its approval, as fans stomp their feet on the bleachers in a deafening roar.

The ball is set again, the blockers go up, the hitter swings away, and the ball is blocked, falling back on the hitter's side of the court. The setter makes a spectacular save and the play continues.

The audience is cheering wildly. The spectators can't believe the ball is still in the air. The ball is set again, and this time the hitter taps the ball over the hands of the blockers. The off blocker sees the tip just in time and rushes in to make the play, but he hits the ball into the net. Not to worry, the setter slides under the ball, waits for it to come off the net, and bumps it back up into the air before it can touch the ground. The outside hitter leaps into the air and smashes

Forearm pass: Forearms together, elbows in, shoulders up and out.

Concentration: Head up, watch the ball come off your arms.

Knee pads: For dropping down on one knee to dig low balls.

Move to the ball, keep your weight on the balls of your feet.

Digging out the ball is just one of the quick, reflexive moves a player learns when playing volleyball.

the ball between the hands of the blockers, sending it sailing across court. There, the best defensive player on the team is waiting to dig the ball and set up the next play.

The setter gently sets the ball to a middle position, where two hitters seem to go after the same ball. The first hitter jumps early and fakes a hit. The blockers react by jumping into the air with the first hitter. But it is the second hitter who smashes the ball into an open corner of the court for the game-winning point.

The team goes wild. High fives, hugging, screams of joy, and a chant, "We're number one!" signals the crowning of the championship team.

This is the fast-paced game of volleyball; a team sport where the skills of the individual combine on the court to make a winning team. Who were those six players who just won the championship game? Were they boys or girls, men or women, youngsters, teenagers or adults—or maybe even Olympic athletes? It could be any of them.

Today, volleyball is played by people of all ages and skill levels. It is one of the hottest, youngest, fastest-growing sports in America.

Volleyball is not just one game; it is several games. Volleyball can be played indoors on hardwood floors, outdoors on grass, and on sand at the beach. Teams can be made up of six, four, or even two people.

The indoor game is usually made up of teams of six players each. Grass volleyball tournaments' teams are made up of two, four, or six players. Often there are different categories such as two men, two women, or co-ed where teams are made up of one man and one woman.

Beach volleyball is played on the sand, but not always at the beach. Many parks, sports clubs, and schools now build their own "beach" by digging a huge square pit and filling it with sand. One beach volleyball tournament was held in the middle of a huge parking lot where thousands of tons of sand were brought in by the truckload to make the sand volleyball courts.

The most popular beach volleyball game is the "two-man" game, where two players on each team try to cover the same size court as six players cover on the indoor court. The action is fast and constant, with each player performing all the volleyball skills.

Professional beach volleyball has been built around the two-person game consisting of a series of tournaments for both women and men. Four-person beach volleyball is also gaining popularity with both men and women because, with more people on the court, the ball stays in play longer. This game is similar to the indoor game where two players can block at the net and teams can run a variety of hitting plays.

Beach volleyball today is just as popular as indoor, Olympic-style volleyball.

In two-person volleyball, it is easy to guess who will be hitting the ball: the person who passed the ball to the setter. The setter only has one person he or she can set to; but in four person volleyball, there are three other people who are allowed to hit the ball.

Not only are there a number of different playing surfaces (hardwood floor, sand and grass) in volleyball and a variety of player combinations (two, three, four or six), there are also several skill levels. The beginner level can be seen at the Saturday afternoon game at the park, and the skill levels go up from there, all the way to the Olympics and professional volleyball.

Many people get their first taste of volleyball in a backyard or park where someone has set up a net. Volleyball players can be found at family birthday parties, company picnics, the local park and beaches, and on the blacktop at school.

Volleyball at school often starts in physical education class or during recess. Many students who find the game fun will try out for the school volleyball team. Junior high and high schools often have volleyball teams and compete against other schools in their area. Girls' volleyball has been a popular fall sport

Volleyball played with just two persons on a team means each player has to be versatile, able to cover a larger area of the court.

for a number of years, but since boys' volleyball competes with baseball in the spring, it is not played at all schools. Schools located near the ocean and beaches usually have boys' volleyball teams because the students there are more familiar with the sport.

Volleyball for girls is very popular. Girls' volleyball teams can be found across the country. Almost every high school will have a girls' volleyball team, with many schools having a varsity and junior varsity team. High school volleyball can lead to college volleyball, where a really good high school player can earn a volleyball scholarship to a four-year college. In college, the level of competition is quite high and it can be difficult to make the team.

Girls' and women's volleyball has grown into an intense game of skill and teamwork that makes it exciting for fans as well as players.

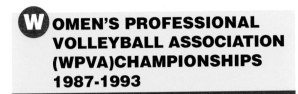

WOMEN'S PROFESSIONAL VOLLEYBALL ASSOCIATION (WPVA) CHAMPIONSHIPS 1987-1993

1993 Karolyn Kirby/Liz Masakayan
      Manhattan Beach, CA

1992 Karolyn Kirby/Nancy Reno
      Manhattan Beach, CA

1991 Linda Carrillo/Liz Masakayan
      Las Vegas, NV

1990 Nina Matthies/Elaine Roque
      Laughlin, NV

1989 Rita Crockett/Jackie Silva
      Will Rogers Park, CA

1988 Linda Carrillo/Jackie Silva
      Pismo Beach, CA

1987 Linda Carrillo/Jackie Silva
      Pismo Beach, CA

Many athletes join volleyball clubs so they can play volleyball all year. Volleyball clubs practice and play games against other volleyball club teams. They also go to tournaments and, if they are very good, will advance to the Junior Olympics.

When volleyball players graduate from college, they can try out for the national team that plays in the Olympics, turn professional and try to win enough tournaments to make a living, or play volleyball on the recreational level—in other words, just for fun.

Volleyball is a sport for all ages and all skill levels. It's for players who want to learn the game as well as for those who have been playing for many years. There are park leagues and tournaments for amateurs who are just learning the game, and professional tournaments where players can win thousands of dollars during a single weekend. The best way to go from a beginner to advanced is to play the game. The more you play, the better you will be.

You don't have to be a big athlete or an adult to enjoy volleyball.

Do You Have What It Takes?

CHAPTER TWO

What makes a good volleyball player? The better players are fast; they move quickly to the ball. They can jump high into the air to block, hit or serve. Good players are strong; they hit the ball hard when they spike. But they also have a soft touch; they can pass or set the ball to the perfect spot every time.

The best players have all these skills, but even these athletes can be great at one skill and not as good at another. Volleyball is a team sport. A volleyball coach may find that some big players are taller and stronger than the others. They will be the blockers and hitters. One athlete may be an excellent setter and another may be great at passing the ball. The coach's job is to find which athletes will be best at each position. Not everyone on the team has to be tall, big, strong, and quick.

One example is Eric Sato, a volleyball player on the United States Men's National Volleyball Team since 1986. At 5-feet, 10

For many years one of the top players in United States men's volleyball has been Eric Sato.

1/2-inches, Eric is the smallest player on the team. Yet he has played on two Olympic volleyball teams and the Gold Medal Pan American team in 1987. He was on the team in 1988 when the U.S. won the gold medal at the Seoul Olympics in Korea. It was Eric's jump serve that gave the United States the winning point in the final match against the Soviet Union. He was also on the U.S. team in 1992 when it won the bronze medal at the Barcelona Olympics in Spain.

Eric Sato has a powerful jump serve and is one of the best defensive players in the back court. He may be small, but he's quick. When Eric rotates to the front row, the coach substitutes in one of the bigger players to hit and block. It doesn't matter that Eric is less than six feet tall because he works on his defensive skills and serve to be the best. "Being smaller, you have to out-think the taller players and keep one step ahead of your opponents," says Sato.

Practice, practice, practice, and a desire to improve and win can make anyone into a decent volleyball player.

The Basics

The game of volleyball starts when one player serves the ball across the net to the other team. Each team tries to win points by making the ball touch the ground on the other team's side of the court. Each team is allowed to touch the ball three times before the ball must go back over the net. A point can only be scored for a team when that team is serving the ball.

If a team wins the rally but wasn't serving at the time, it's called a *sideout*. A sideout means the winning team has won the right to serve. Sometimes teams can play for a long time without either team scoring a point.

This is a typical order of events in a volleyball game: The ball is served, and a player uses a forearm pass to send the ball up in the air to the setter. The setter uses his or her fingertips to set up an overhead pass, sending the ball into the air and close to the net for the hitter. The hitter spikes the ball over the net. These are the first three, basic contacts.

The two most important skills in volleyball are the serve and the forearm pass. If a team can't serve, they will never score a point. If a team can't pass, they will never be able to set up their offense and sideout. A team can play an entire game by just serving the ball over the net and then passing the ball back and forth. The serve and the pass are the first two skills taught to beginning volleyball players.

The Serve

The game always starts with the *serve*. One player stands at the back of the court behind the line, and then hits the ball over the net. It is 30 feet from the back line to the net, so the server must hit the ball hard. Unless a player is rotated out, everyone on the court will have a turn to serve, so everyone needs to learn how to serve.

The serve is the only time in the game when a single player has total and complete control over what happens. All eyes are on the server. Sometimes this makes the server nervous and he or she misses the serve. Having a good serve can help the team win games. Many times one server will score five, ten, or even 15 points in a row. Any serve that can't be returned by the other team is called an ace.

The easiest type of serve to learn is the *underhand serve*. The ball is held in one hand, away from and in front of the body. The player takes one step forward and swings the other hand under the ball, hitting it out of the hand with the fist and over the net.

The underhand serve (left) or the overhand serve (right) puts the ball in play. Every member of the team must learn at least one type of serve.

The *overhand serve* is a little harder to learn but it is also a more difficult serve for the other team to return. The server tosses the ball into the air instead of holding the ball in the hand, takes the same step forward, and reaches up with the hitting arm and smacks the ball before it drops. This serve is similar to the serve used in tennis.

The *jump ball* is a spectacular serve that can be very hard to return. Not everyone can jump serve. The server tosses the ball into the air, but this time the toss is much higher than a regular overhand serve. The server takes two steps forward and jumps into the air as high as possible, hitting the ball while it is in the air. A good hard jump serve ball seems to barely clear the net before it makes a dive to the floor.

The *sky ball* is an underhand serve that is only used outdoors. The server hits the ball as high into the air as possible. Players on the other team have to wait a long time for the ball to come down. The wind may blow the ball around a lot as it descends. This makes it a hard serve to return.

Many players learn to master more than one type of serve so they can choose the one that will work best against the team they are playing.

The Pass

After one team serves the ball over the net, the other team will try to stop it and pass it up to the *setter*, who is standing close to the net. This skill is called the *forearm pass* and is an important part of the game. If the passers don't stop the serve, the other team will score points. If the passers don't get the ball to the setter, there will be no chance for a set and a spike.

The forearm pass starts when the player moves in front of the ball. With hands clasped together, the passer contacts the ball with the forearms, between the wrists and elbows, and directs it to the setter.

The Set

The *set* or overhead pass is usually performed by the setter, but everyone on the team should be able to overhead pass in case the setter can't get to the ball. The setter is always supposed to make the second contact, placing the ball close to the net for the hitters. The overhand pass starts when the setter moves under the ball. Both hands are extended overhead. In slow motion, it looks as if the player catches the ball with the fingers and then throws it up into the air again. Many coaches teach their players how to overhead pass by having them catch the ball over their head and then throwing it up again. By repeating this over and over, faster and faster, players learn to set the ball.

The Spike

Many spectators think the *spike* is the most exciting part of volleyball. This is when the hitter jumps up into the air and hits the ball down at the other team as hard as possible. Hitters must back away from the net before they can spike as they need plenty of room. A hitter takes two or three running steps, swings his or her arms, then leaps straight up into the air. The hitting arm is held high, elbow bent, ready to hit

Learning how to set is just as important as serving. The set is an overhead pass that moves the ball into position for the hitters who return the ball over the net.

the ball while the player is still in the air. Everyone wants to be the big hitter, but it takes a good pass and set before the hitter has a chance to put the ball away.

"I couldn't even spike the ball in my first two years of high school," says professional beach volleyball player Sinjin Smith. "I just didn't develop physically right away. But if you develop your other skills at a young age then it becomes second nature to you. When you finally do develop physically then you'll have a head start on the other players."

These are the basic skills needed to play volleyball. An elementary or junior high school team can do well if it just masters these skills. But as players get better, grow taller, become stronger and move on to high school, college, and club teams, there are a number of advanced skills they will need to know.

The spike may be the most dramatic moment during any game, where the opposing team must block the speeding ball from hitting the court.

Advanced Skills

To win a volleyball game, a team must learn how to stop the opposing team's big hitters from pounding the ball down on their side of the court. One way to do this is to *block* the hit. To block, players stand at the net and wait for the hitter to jump up in the air for the spike. Then the blockers jump straight up at the net and try to stop the ball with their hands from coming over the net.

If the hitter can hit the ball over or around the block, then it's up to the back court to *dig* the ball before it can touch the ground. To dig the ball, players need to get low and move quickly to the ball. Good defensive players will dive or slide to save a ball from hitting the ground.

When the blockers are making one great block after another, the hitter will sometimes *dink* the ball over the top of the block. A dink is when the hitter uses his or her hitting hand to gently tip the ball over the block instead of spiking it.

There are a number of other advanced skills. Many involve special offensive plays where the hitters are moving to special areas on the court. One team is always trying to catch the other off guard so it can score a point. Once a player learns the basic skills, it is easier to become part of a team where advanced techniques are being used.

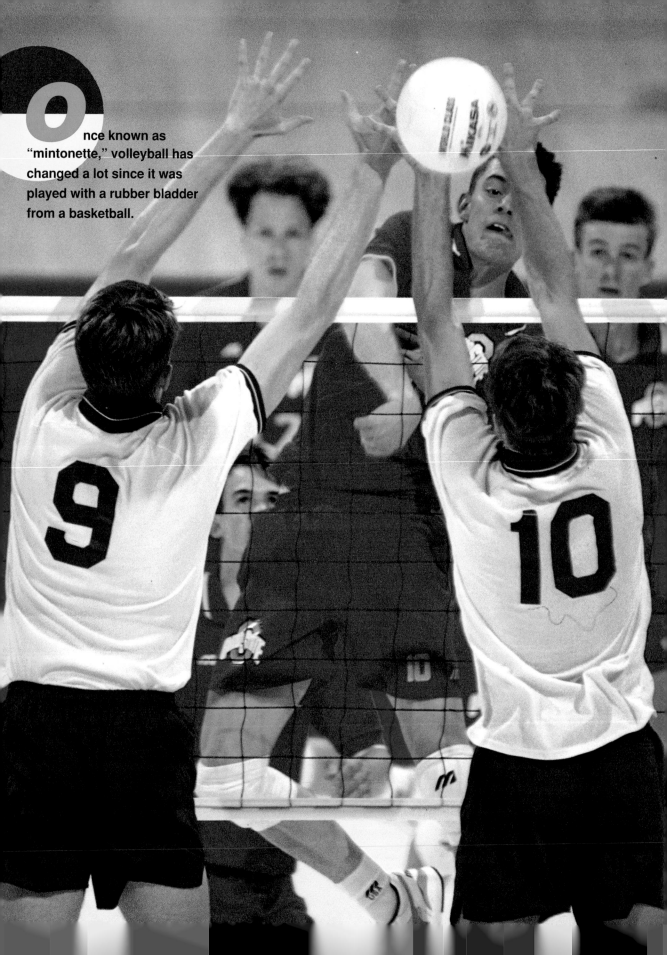

Once known as "mintonette," volleyball has changed a lot since it was played with a rubber bladder from a basketball.

How It All Began

It is estimated that over 30 million people played volleyball in the United States in 1992. Today, students at school, adults in leagues, college teams, beach teams, pro players, and amateurs all enjoy a game that was invented in Massachusetts back in 1895.

A physical education director at the Holyoke YMCA named William G. Morgan wanted to find a game that was easier to play than basketball. Since basketball was too much work for many people, Morgan invented a new game he called *mintonette.*

Mintonette was very different from today's version of volleyball. A team could have as many players on the court at one time as it wanted. The players could hit the ball five, six, or even ten times before it had to go back over the net. The net was very low—only 6-feet 6-inches. Today's net for men's volleyball is almost 8 feet high. There was no special ball for volleyball, so teams played with the rubber bladder from the inside of a basketball.

Since the name mintonette didn't describe the game, Morgan changed the name to volleyball because the ball is "volleyed" back and forth across the net. Through the years many changes were made to improve the game. The Spaulding Company designed the first official volleyball. New rules were made, and the net height was raised.

During World Wars I and II, United States troops played volleyball for fun throughout Europe, thereby introducing the sport to the world. By 1947, the first international volleyball organization was formed to promote international competitions and make the game rules the same around the world.

The first time volleyball was played in the Olympics was at the 1964 games in Tokyo, Japan. The teams from the United States however, did not do

Volleyball is a big team sport in the Olympics. This game from the 1992 Barcelona Games is between the women's teams of China and Cuba.

so well. Even though volleyball was invented in the United States it wasn't until 20 years later that a U.S. team finally won a gold medal. At the 1984 Olympics in Los Angeles, the men's national team defeated the team from Brazil in the final match of the competition. The U.S. women's team also played well, earning the second place silver medal.

Beach Volleyball

While high school, college, and national teams were pounding the ball indoors, another group of volleyball players were taking the game to the beach. Four players would battle it out in the sun and sand, just for the right to say they won. There was no prize money awarded to the winners, no sponsors or television coverage, just thousands of cheering fans.

During the 1940s, '50s and '60s, beach volleyball was just a bunch of guys who loved to play. Two-man teams would drive up and down the California coast, from one tournament to another, just to play volleyball. It wasn't until the

1976 World Championships that prize money was awarded to the winning team.

Beach volleyball finally caught on. In 1983, the beach volleyball players came together to form the AVP: the Association of Volleyball Professionals. One year later, the top players went on strike and refused to play in the World Championships because the company that was hired to run the AVP wasn't allowing the players any say in the running of the games. The strike was a big success. In a very short time, the players went from having no control over the sport to having almost total control. Today, professional beach volleyball is one of the few sports where the players control how the game is played.

VOLLEYBALL IN SCHOOL

In elementary and high schools, volleyball became the girls' major fall sport. While boys were playing football, girls were being taught volleyball. School volleyball leagues and tournaments were held each season and the winning teams were crowned champions. Since boys in high school played football and not volleyball, many people thought that volleyball was just for girls.

College women had been playing volleyball for 54 years before they finally had their first chance to play in a national volleyball championship. The first United States championship for women took place in Los Angeles, California in 1949. The first women's world championship followed three years later and was held in Moscow.

When beach volleyball first began, tournaments were held only in California. Then Clearwater Beach in Florida became a tournament stop, and so Florida was introduced to professional beach volleyball.

Today, professional beach volleyball tournaments are held in cities like Philadelphia, Pennsylvania; Chicago, Illinois; Belmar, New Jersey; and Phoenix, Arizona. Ten years after the formation of the Association of Volleyball Professionals, the AVP Tour has grown into a professional sport where athletes can make a living playing volleyball. In 1993, the AVP tour visited 14 states, was aired on national television, and handed out $3 million in total prize money. Not too bad for a bunch of guys who started out playing volleyball on the beach.

Beach volleyball is still growing. Indoor sand courts are being built in places thousands of miles away from the beach. Now volleyball players in places like Rochester, New York, can play beach volleyball inside while it is snowing outside.

Beach volleyball is growing around the world, too. There is even a Beach World Series. Players travel around the world to places like Hiroshima,

Beach volleyball is now a professional sport with tournaments played throughout the United States.

Japan; Sydney, Australia; and Copacabana, Brazil; to play against beach volleyball teams from other countries. Beach volleyball has become so successful that it will soon be an official Olympic event. Two-man beach volleyball teams will come from around the world to "Go for the Gold" at the 1996 Summer Olympic Games to be held in Atlanta, Georgia.

Men are not the only ones playing professional beach volleyball. Two-woman professional beach volleyball started in 1987. The Women's Professional Volleyball Association, the WPVA, organizes tournaments and promotes the women's beach volleyball tour. Although the prize money and television coverage is not as great as that of the men's tour, the action on the court is still as hot as sand in summer.

Four-Person Beach Volleyball

Four-person beach volleyball is the newest form of the game. The first four-man tour hit the beach in 1991. The four-woman tour is even newer, with its first season starting in May of 1993. Many of the players on the four-person teams used to play on the U.S. national team and played in the Olympics.

It takes a great deal of stamina to play volleyball on a shifting court surface of sand.

In four-person beach volleyball, there are more rallies. With more players on the court, teams can have two people blocking and still have two people to cover the back of the court. The fans love the action of four-person volleyball. In 1993, there were five men's teams and five women's teams that played in ten different tournaments around the country. The players hope that as the sport grows, four-person beach volleyball will become as popular with the fans as the two-person version of the sport.

Volleyball Drills

Volleyball is a game of skill. Players who wish to become better volleyball players must spend time practicing the individual volleyball skills like the serve, the set, and the pass. Team practice, of course, provides you with lots of opportunities to improve your technique and your ability to work together with other players. But working on your skills alone is just as important. In baseball, you can take batting practice; in volleyball, the drills are just as specialized.

Volleyball coaches use a number of drills to practice each technique. The purpose of a drill is to repeat the same skill over and over again. In this way the player can concentrate on each individual skill before putting them all together in a game situation. Many of the drills volleyball coaches use with their teams can be used by individual players on their own to improve their playing skills. The following are a few volleyball drills that can be practiced by yourself without a volleyball court.

The Serve

One of the most important parts of a good overhand serve is the toss. When you toss the ball up to serve it, it shouldn't have any spin on it. The volleyball should only be tossed one foot in the air and, if the ball is allowed to drop, land next to your left foot and in front of your right shoulder (if you're right handed). The following directions are for right handers; if you're left handed, just reverse the directions.

Practice your toss by standing with your left foot in front, arms stretched out holding the ball at shoulder height. Toss the ball 10 to 12 inches into the air with as little spin on the ball as possible. Let the ball drop. If the ball lands to the right of your left foot in front of your right shoulder, then you made a good toss. Repeat this drill 20 times.

After you have perfected the toss, you are ready to hit the ball. Stand 15 feet away from an outdoor wall. It could be the side of your house, a handball court, or a brick wall. Toss the ball, step forward with your left foot as you hit the ball with your right hand held high above your head. By using the wall, each of your serves should come back to you and you won't have to chase the ball. If the ball hits the wall about eight feet high (or higher) and comes straight back, then the serve would have gone over the net. Repeat this skill 50 times. Yes, 50! Serving is a skill that only improves with hundreds of repetitions.

The Set

The set is another skill players can practice on their own. To build strength in their fingers, many setters will practice setting with a heavier ball like a basketball. Hold the basketball at forehead height, cradled in your fingers. Flick the ball straight up, above your head, by extending your arms and pushing the ball away with your fingertips. Catch the ball above your head and repeat over and over.

To practice a light touch as well as accuracy, use a basketball hoop as a target while setting a volleyball. A high arching set is needed to make a basket. Start in front of the free throw line and set the ball to the hoop. Once you can make baskets from that position, move further back and change angles. Rebounds don't count. Good setters must be able to place the ball in the perfect spot for the hitters.

The Pass

To practice passing without a partner you'll need to use a wall again. Toss the ball at the wall and be ready to pass the ball as it bounces off. Count how many times you can pass the ball in a row before the ball touches the ground. It takes control and fast feet to keep the ball in play. If you have a partner you can still use the wall by alternating passes.

Sinjin Smith
is one of the best
beach volleyball
players of the '90s.

Famous Players, Teams, and Tournaments

Every sport has its famous players and great teams. Baseball has Babe Ruth, Barry Bonds, and Nolan Ryan. Basketball has Michael Jordan and Shaquille O'Neal. Who are the famous volleyball players? What are the best teams and most prestigious tournaments?

In the early '60s, "Team Mike" was the dominant beach volleyball team. Mike O'Hara and Mike Bright won five straight Manhattan Beach Open titles from 1960 through 1964.

"Team Ron," made up of Ron Von Hagen and Ron Lang, played for a year-and-a-half against all the best beach volleyball players and never lost a single game or tournament. This winning streak included back-to-back wins at the Manhattan Beach Open in 1966 and 1967.

The number one team of the '70s was Jim Menges and Greg Lee, winning a record 13 straight tournaments. They also won the 1975 and 1978 Manhattan Beach Open and the first ever World Championship. When Greg Lee left volleyball to play pro basketball in Germany, Jim Menges went on to win three other Manhattan Beach Opens with other partners.

If the '70s belonged to Menges and Lee, then the '80s belonged to two teams: Smith & Stoklos, and Hovland & Dodd.

Sinjin Smith and Randy Stoklos are the best known volleyball players today, and for good reason. Smith and Stoklos have won more games together as a team than any other beach volleyball team. As of 1993, Sinjin Smith was ranked number one in all-time career wins with 133, and Randy Stoklos was the first player to earn over $1 million playing beach volleyball. In their 12 years together, they won 115 tournaments including the U.S. World Championship titles in 1982, 1985, and 1988. They also won at Manhattan Beach in 1986 and 1989. No other team has ever won so many tournaments together!

In May of 1993, the best beach volleyball team of all time split up. Both Sinjin Smith and Randy Stoklos are now playing with new partners. But it will be a long time before another team can break their incredible record.

Tim Hovland and Mike Dodd dominated the Manhattan Beach Open, winning in 1982, '83, '84, '85 and again in 1987. The World Championships also belonged to Hovland and Dodd with wins in 1983, '86, '87, and '89.

In the early '90s, Karch Kiraly and Kent Steffes exploded onto the beach volleyball scene. Together they tied Jim Menges and Greg Lee's record of 13 straight tournament wins, including the 1991 and 1992 Manhattan Beach Open. Karch Kiraly was a four-time All-American and won three NCAA Championships at UCLA. He also was on both the U.S. Olympic teams that won the gold medal. Kent Steffes, at the age of 24, became the youngest player to be ranked number one in beach volleyball.

When Karch Kiraly won the 1993 Manhattan Beach Open, he became the first player to ever win six Manhattan Beach Opens. Kiraly won with four different partners: Sinjin Smith, Ricci Luyties, Brent Frohoff and Kent Steffes.

The world of women's professional beach volleyball has its great players, too. The first year that the women's tour hit the beaches, the team of Linda Carrillo and Jackie Silva was practically unbeatable. Out of ten tournaments, Carrillo and Silva won eight, with Carrillo winning a ninth tournament with another partner.

In 1988, this same team won seven out of nine tournaments. Changing partners the next year, Jackie Silva teamed up with Patty Dodd to win 11 out of 15 tournaments including nine in a row. Today, Jackie Silva has the most career wins at 41 after winning 39 of the first 50 tournaments between 1987 and 1990.

Karolyn Kirby is the tour's all-time money winner with 36 career wins so far. In 1991, Karolyn Kirby, with partner Angela Rock, set a Women's Professional Volleyball Association record for the most victories in a single season. Kirby and Rock won 12 of 17 events in one year. By the middle of 1992, they broke another women's record with 17 career wins together. Changing partners in 1993, Karolyn Kirby teamed up with Liz Masakayan to win eight of the first nine events with only four tournaments left to play in the '93 season.

One of the most popular volleyball tournaments on the pro circuit is the Manhattan Beach Open in California.

Liz Masakayan was a two-time All-American at U.C.L.A and a member of the U.S. National Team for five years before she started playing beach volleyball. As a member of the National Team, Liz won three bronze and one silver medal. On the beach, she was awarded the WPVA Most Valuable Player in 1992 and Best Defensive Player in 1991 and '92.

Famous Tournaments

Most players will agree that if a team hasn't won a Manhattan Beach Open, they haven't really made it to the top. That's how much this tournament means to the players. It's not the money that makes this a great tournament. There are several tournaments where the winners take home bigger checks, but even without the dollars, this is still the tournament everyone wants to win. Maybe it's because the Manhattan Beach Open is the oldest beach volleyball tournament around. The first tournament, held in 1960, was won by "Team Mike": Mike O'Hara and Mike Bright.

The Manhattan Beach Open is the only stop on the AVP tour where anybody can sign up to play. Here's how it works. There are 64 total teams —48 pro and 16 amateur. There is a 32-team amateur field where anyone can enter. If an amateur team wins one match, they become one of the 16 amateur teams in the Manhattan Beach Open. It is possible for a completely unknown team to end up playing against Sinjin Smith, Karch Kiraly, or Tim Hovland.

NCAA women's volleyball teams provide outstanding displays of collegiate athletic competition.

The U.S. Championships of men's professional beach volleyball is the World Series of beach volleyball. It is one of the few volleyball tournaments televised live. When this tournament first started in 1976, its prize money was only $5,000. In 1993, this tournament handed out $250,000 in prize money.

The Most Famous Coach

UCLA men's volleyball coach Al Scates is the winningest volleyball coach in college history. His UCLA teams were NCAA Volleyball Champions 14 times from 1970 to 1993. He was the head coach of the U.S. Olympic team in 1972 and the Pan American team in 1971. Coach Scates also led the national team to three USVBA Championships.

FAMOUS INDOOR TEAMS

The 1976-77 University of Southern California (USC) women's volleyball team has the only perfect season in women's collegiate volleyball. Their record was an incredible 38-0, including the National Championships.

The University of California at Los Angeles (UCLA) had three undefeated men's college volleyball teams: the 1979 team, the 1982 team, and the 1984 team. During each of those years, the UCLA men's team won the NCAA National Championship.

The 1993 Washington (Missouri) University Women's team became the first NCAA Division III team to finish with an undefeated record of 40-0, including the Championships. The year before, the team had lost only six games all season. Five players from the Washington team were named All-Americans. This was the first time five players from the same team were elected All-Americans.

Both the men's and women's U.S. volleyball teams were contenders for medals at the 1992 Olympic Games in Barcelona.

Going for the Gold

Do you ever dream of playing volleyball in the Olympics? If you do, you are not alone. When Eric Sato was in junior high school, he wanted more than anything to be on the Olympic volleyball team.

"I didn't think I would be," said Sato. But he did make the Olympic team. He played on the 1988 gold medal team and the 1992 bronze medal team. Dreams can come true.

U.S. Olympic volleyball wasn't always a dream team. In fact, in the beginning it was more of a nightmare. The first year volleyball was an Olympic event was in 1964. Since the sport was invented in the United States, many people thought the U.S. team would do well, maybe even bring home a medal. Sadly, it was not to be. The men's team finished ninth out of the ten teams competing. Their record was two wins and seven losses.

Up through 1992, the U.S. women's volleyball team had one silver medal and four bronze medals in international tournaments. Here they face off against a team from Japan.

The women's team didn't play much better. The players knew they were in big trouble when they held a practice game against a Japanese high school team and lost. They ended up finishing fifth out of six teams.

It really wasn't the players' fault that the U.S. teams did so poorly. Volleyball wasn't considered to be an important sport in the United States like it was in other countries. Both the 1964 men's and women's teams were given only two weeks of practice before going to the Olympics, while teams from other countries practiced all year. The Japanese women's team practiced eight hours a day, seven days a week. They even had practice on holidays. In Japan, volleyball players were famous people. In America, volleyball players were unknowns.

One player on the U.S. women's team, a schoolteacher, had money taken out of her paycheck because she missed two weeks of work to go to the Olympics. In China and the Soviet Union, volleyball players were given help and special jobs that allowed them to practice and earn a living at the same time.

If the United States wanted to win an Olympic medal in volleyball, they needed to make some changes. A national training center was set up in San Diego, California, so that the teams had a place to practice all year. Players were given small salaries so they could play volleyball and work part-time. The national team played in tournaments against teams from other countries, which helped them improve their skills. The coaches changed the offensive and defensive strategies to make them more competitive.

It took a long time, but 20 years after the first Olympic volleyball event, both the men's and women's teams finally won their first Olympic medals. The men's team won the gold medal and the women's team won the silver medal at the 1984 Olympic Games held in Los Angeles.

This was the beginning of a world class volleyball program for the United States. Between 1982 and 1992, the women's team won one silver medal and four bronze medals in international competitions. During the same time period, the men's team won five gold medals, one silver, and one bronze medal.

Between 1985 and 1988, the United States men's volleyball team was the best in the world. What made this team so special?

"One thread that ran through this gold medal team was they played volleyball eight days a week. There was volleyball in their blood," says Marv Dunphy, head coach of the 1988 U.S. Men's Gold Medal Team and head coach at Pepperdine University in Malibu, California.

"We weren't the biggest, fastest, or strongest, but we were the best. I think that this team was one of the most competitive volleyball teams in the history of the sport," says Coach Dunphy.

Today, not only do the national teams play year-round, they also play around the world. The World League tour has made stops in Russia, Japan, Germany, Brazil, Greece, and the United States. The tour gives all the teams a

Marv Dunphy, head coach of the gold medal-winning U.S. men's volleyball team at the 1988 Seoul Olympics.

Bryan Ivie spikes the ball for Team USA.

chance to practice against the best in the world. National teams from around the world participate in the Olympics, the World Championships, and the World Cup competitions. Countries from North and South America also participate in the Pan American games, which are held every two years.

Your Road to the Olympics

Back in 1961, Japan did not have a winning men's volleyball team. That year they lost 122 matches. So the Japanese coach, Matsudaira, made some changes. His goal was to win a gold medal in volleyball. Ten years later at the 1972 Munich Olympics his team did just that.

One of the changes he made involved moms! He started what was called "Mama's Volleyball." Coach Matsudaira thought that if mothers learned how to play volleyball they could teach their children, and if children started playing volleyball when they were young, they would become better volleyball players later. Soon the entire country was playing volleyball.

The idea of having children learn a sport at an early age is not new. In countries where young people ski to school every day, great skiers emerge. In countries where everyone plays soccer as soon as they can kick a ball, great soccer teams are born.

The United States Volleyball Association (USVBA) realized that to have gold medal national teams, the United States needed children to start playing volleyball as early as possible. So starting in 1980, the USVBA began providing recreational programs through the YMCA and community parks. Camps and competitions for young players aged 7 to 26 began popping up everywhere. Today, USA Youth Volleyball programs across the country are

Young people can learn to play volleyball—even learn to spike the ball—at any age.

teaching children how to play the game. Boys and girls age 11 to 18 can compete in the U.S. Junior Olympics held every year when over 200 teams come together to play volleyball.

Of all the participants in the Junior Olympics, 72 of the best players are chosen to attend the Elite Junior National Training Camp. Here the young athletes work at becoming even better volleyball players.

At the college level, the best young men and women have a chance to attend the Senior Elite Camp and try out for the Olympic Festival team and the World University Games. All of these camps, programs, and competitions are designed to help good players become great.

The Future and You

Imagine this: Michael Jordan and Charles Barkley are playing a one-on-one basketball game at the park near your house. People are sitting around watching, cheering, and retrieving balls for the famous players. After the game, Michael and Charles sign a few autographs and talk to the fans before calling it a day. Wouldn't that be something to see?

HOW TO BECOME A GREAT PLAYER

Olympic volleyball coach Marv Dunphy has a few tips for young people who dream of playing volleyball for the national team.

• Play volleyball with kids who are better than you. This will make you work harder and play better.

• Try out for any team that has open tryouts. Even if you don't make the team, the experience will teach you a lot.

• The one thing that will improve your volleyball skills more than anything else is to play, play, PLAY!

"I grew up at the beach," says beach volleyball great Sinjin Smith. "As a kid, I was able to see the very best volleyball players play. They were bigger than life; they were my heroes. I watched football, basketball, and baseball on television but that didn't leave nearly the impression as seeing these guys in real life. That left a huge impression on me as an 8-year-old kid."

One of the great things about the sport of volleyball is that the game is still fairly new, so fans can get a close look at their heroes. For example, it is still possible to go to a professional beach tournament and sit in the sand right next to the court. Most players will sign autographs, agree to have their pictures taken, and even talk with the fans after their games.

As a career for professional athletes, however, volleyball has a lot of catching up to do to reach the status of other professional sports. For example, not one volleyball player made it to the list of the world's 40 highest-paid professional athletes. While volleyball players will probably never make as much money as baseball or basketball players, today's top players are beginning to break the million-dollar mark.

As more volleyball players start to show up at the park, on the beach, in the gym, and even in television commercials, people will become more aware of the sport. Beach volleyball tournaments are being played across the country, not just in California, and beach tournaments and indoor matches are being shown on television. Sports fans of all ages will now have a chance to see great volleyball in action.

Volleyball is growing quickly and anyone can become a part of the action. The Federation of Outdoor Volleyball Associations (FOVA) is a national organization of event directors who run recreational tournaments for amateur players. They run sand and grass tournaments for men's teams, women's teams, and youth teams. There are 25 FOVA headquarters located in various states across the United States including: Arizona, Arkansas, California, Connecticut, Florida, Kentucky, Tennessee, Texas, Utah, Vermont, and Wisconsin. Players interested in local outdoor volleyball tournaments should call the FOVA headquarters in their area.

For those who prefer indoor volleyball, there are club teams, the YMCA, park and recreation teams, and the USVBA. The USVBA is a good place to start. Their offices can provide information on local clubs, clinics, and organizations that sponsor youth volleyball teams and programs.

Volleyball summer camp is a great way to learn a lot about playing the game in a short period of time. Most of the camps are less than a week long: some are sleep-over camps, and others are day camps. Many of the bigger, college

Bob Samuelson and Steve Timmons celebrate a victory during the 1992 Olympic Games in Barcelona.

UNITED STATES VOLLEYBALL ASSOCIATION (USVBA) WOMEN'S AND MEN'S NATIONAL TEAM ACHIEVEMENTS

WOMEN	MEN
World Championships Bronze 1982, 1990	**World Cup** Gold 1985
Pan American Games Bronze 1987	**World Championships** Gold 1986
Olympic Games Silver 1984 Bronze 1992	**Pan American Games** Gold 1987 Silver 1991
	Olympic Games Gold 1984, 1988 Bronze 1992

camps are run by some of the best volleyball coaches in the country. Those who really love volleyball are wild about volleyball camp, where the game is played from early in the morning until late at night. Some players are known to even take their volleyball to bed with them. At volleyball camp there is no such thing as too much volleyball.

For those who want to play on their school team, at the beach or in the Olympics, there's only one piece of advice they need. Olympic star Eric Sato, Olympic Coach Marv Dunphy, and beach volleyball legend Sinjin Smith all say the same thing: the best way to improve is to play, play, play. So grab a volleyball and a few friends and pass, set, spike!

Glossary

Ace. Any type of serve that is not returned by the other team. An ace serve is always a point.

Association of Volleyball Professionals (AVP). This is the organization which runs men's professional beach volleyball.

Block. A defensive player jumps up at the net and stops the ball from being hit over the net.

Dig. When the ball has been spiked, the defensive player will stop the ball from hitting the ground using one or two arms. This is called digging the ball.

Dink. When a player lightly tips the ball over the block instead of hitting the ball hard, it's called a dink.

Forearm pass. Players use their forearms to contact the ball after the serve. The ball is passed up to the setter using the forearm pass. The forearm pass is also called a bump.

Federation of Outdoor Volleyball Association (FOVA). This is a group that organizes outdoor amateur volleyball tournaments.

Jump serve. The jump serve is an advanced skill where the player tosses the ball in the air and then jumps up to hit the ball across the net.

Mintonette. The name William Morgan first used to describe the game of volleyball.

Overhand serve. A type of serve where the ball is tossed in the air and hit with the hand raised above the head.

Overhead pass. A type of set where the player uses two hands to contact the ball above the head to send the ball to a target.

Set. Normally, the second contact of the ball. The set is when a player sets the ball up in position for the hitter to spike the ball. There is an overhead set and a bump set.

Sideout. This occurs when the non-serving team wins a rally and earns the right to serve.

Sky ball. A high underhand serve used in outdoor volleyball. The ball is hit as high as possible so that the wind will make the ball move around before coming down.

Spike. Also called a hit, kill or attack. The spike is usually the third contact made. The ball is spiked when the player jumps into the air and hits the ball down hard at the other team with one hand.

Underhand serve. A type of serve where the ball is held with one hand and hit with the other. The ball is not tossed in the air and is hit at waist level.

United States Volleyball Association (USVBA). The national organization responsible for developing volleyball in the United States from youth programs all the way to the national team.

Women's Professional Volleyball Association (WPVA). The organization responsible for organizing and running the women's professional beach volleyball tours and activities.

For Additional Information

The best place to look for current volleyball information is in one of the two monthly volleyball magazines: *Volleyball* magazine and *Volleyball Monthly*. Both magazines are published in California. They run schedules of local amateur tournaments as well as the professional beach volleyball schedule and the national team schedule. They also carry an annual guide to where the best volleyball summer camps are held.

You can also contact these organizations:

United States Volleyball Association (USVBA). The national organization responsible for developing volleyball in the United States from youth programs all the way to the national team.

Women's Professional Volleyball Association (WPVA). The organization responsible for organizing and running the women's professional beach volleyball tours and activities.

Other Volleyball books you can read include:

Championship Volleyball by Karch Kiraly. Simon and Schuster, 1990.

Pass, Set, Crush: Volleyball Illustrated by Jeff Lucas. Euclid Northwest Publications, 1988.

Winning Volleyball by Allen E. Scates. Allyn & Bacon, 1976.

Better Volleyball for Girls by George Sullivan. Dodd, Mead, 1979.

Index